A Dissertation on Liberty and Necessity, Pleasure and Pain

(1725)

by

Benjamin Franklin

Rise of Douai

ISBN-13: 978-1494918842

ISBN-10: 1494918846

About the Author

A Dissertation on Liberty and Necessity, Pleasure and Pain is an essay by Benjamin Franklin, a founder of the United States.

A noted polymath, Franklin was a leading author, printer, political theorist, politician, postmaster, scientist, musician, inventor, satirist, civic activist, statesman, and diplomat. As a scientist, he was a major figure in the American Enlightenment and the history of physics for his discoveries and theories regarding electricity. He invented the lightning rod, bifocals, the Franklin stove, a carriage odometer, and the glass 'armonica'. He facilitated many civic organizations, including a fire department and a university.

Franklin earned the title of "The First American" for his early and indefatigable campaigning for colonial unity; as an author and spokesman in London for several colonies, then as the first United States Ambassador to France, he exemplified the emerging American nation. Franklin was foundational in defining the American ethos as a marriage of the practical values of thrift, hard work, education, community spirit, self-governing institutions, and opposition to authoritarianism both political and religious, with the scientific and tolerant values of the Enlightenment. In the words of historian Henry Steele Commager, "In a Franklin could be merged the virtues of Puritanism without its defects, the illumination of the Enlightenment without its heat." To Walter Isaacson, this makes Franklin "the most accomplished American of his age and the most influential in inventing the type of society America would become."

Franklin, always proud of his working class roots, became a successful newspaper editor and printer in Philadelphia, the leading city in the colonies. He was also partners with William Goddard and Joseph Galloway the three of whom published the Pennsylvania Chronicle, a newspaper that was known for its revolutionary sentiments and criticisms of the British monarchy in the American colonies. He became wealthy publishing Poor Richard's Almanack and The Pennsylvania Gazette.

Franklin gained international renown as a scientist for his famous experiments in electricity and for his many inventions, especially the lightning rod. He played a major role in establishing the University of Pennsylvania and was elected the first president of the American Philosophical Society. Franklin became a national hero in America when he spearheaded the effort to have Parliament repeal the unpopular Stamp Act. An accomplished diplomat, he was widely admired among the French as American minister to Paris and was a major figure in the development of positive Franco-American relations. His efforts to secure support for the American revolution by shipments of crucial supply to the British Colony through associations with Marquis de Lafayette and other prominent French aristocrats of the time have made him a prominent figure, also as a strategist.

A Dissertation on Liberty and Necessity, Pleasure and Pain

Whatever is, is in its Causes just
Since all Things are by Fate; but purblind Man
Sees but a part o' th' Chain, the nearest Link,
His Eyes not carrying to the equal Beam
That poises all above.
Dryd.

To Mr. J. R.

SIR,

I have here, according to your Request, given you my present Thoughts of the general State of Things in the Universe. Such as they are, you have them, and are welcome to 'em; and if they yield you any Pleasure or Satisfaction, I shall think my Trouble sufficiently compensated. I know my Scheme will be liable to many Objections from a less discerning Reader than your self; but it is not design'd for those who can't understand it. I need not give you any Caution to distinguish the hypothetical Parts of the Argument from the conclusive: You will easily perceive what I design for Demonstration, and what for Probability only. The whole I leave entirely to you, and shall value my self more or less on this account, in proportion to your Esteem and Approbation.

SECT. I. Of Liberty and Necessity.

I. There is said to be a First Mover, who is called GOD, Maker of the Universe.

II. He is said to be all-wise, all-good, all powerful.

These two Propositions being allow'd and asserted by People of almost every Sect and Opinion; I have here suppos'd them granted, and laid them down as the Foundation of my Argument; What follows then, being a Chain of Consequences truly drawn from them, will stand or fall as they are true or false.

III. If He is all-good, whatsoever He doth must be good.

IV. If He is all-wise, whatsoever He doth must be wise.

The Truth of these Propositions, with relation to the two first, I think may be justly call'd evident; since, either that infinite Goodness will act what is ill, or infinite Wisdom what is not wise, is too glaring a Contradiction not to be perceiv'd by any Man of common Sense, and deny'd as soon as understood.

V. If He is all-powerful, there can be nothing either existing or acting in the Universe against or without his

Consent; and what He consents to must be good, because He is good; therefore Evil doth not exist.

Unde Malum? has been long a Question, and many of the Learned have perplex'd themselves and Readers to little Purpose in Answer to it. That there are both Things and Actions to which we give the Name of Evil, is not here deny'd, as Pain, Sickness, Want, Theft, Murder, &c. but that these and the like are not in reality Evils, Ills, or Defects in the Order of the Universe, is demonstrated in the next Section, as well as by this and the following Proposition. Indeed, to suppose any Thing to exist or be done, contrary to the Will of the Almighty, is to suppose him not almighty; or that Something (the Cause of Evil) is more mighty than the Almighty; an Inconsistence that I think no One will defend: And to deny any Thing or Action, which he consents to the existence of, to be good, is entirely to destroy his two Attributes of Wisdom and Goodness.

There is nothing done in the Universe, say the Philosophers, but what God either does, or permits to be done. This, as He is Almighty, is certainly true: But what need of this Distinction between doing and permitting? Why, first they take it for granted that many Things in the Universe exist in such a Manner as is not for the best, and that many Actions are done which ought not to be done, or would be better undone; these Things or Actions they cannot ascribe to God as His, because they have already attributed to Him infinite Wisdom and Goodness; Here then is the

Use of the Word Permit; He permits them to be done, say they. But we will reason thus: If God permits an Action to be done, it is because he wants either Power or Inclination to hinder it; in saying he wants Power, we deny Him to be almighty; and if we say Hewants Inclination or Will, it must be, either because He is not Good, or the Action is not evil, (for all Evil is contrary to the Essence of infinite Goodness.) The former is inconsistent with his before-given Attribute of Goodness, therefore the latter must be true.

It will be said, perhaps, that God permits evil Actions to be done, for wise Ends and Purposes. But this Objection destroys itself; for whatever an infinitely good God hath wise Ends in suffering to be, must be good, is thereby made good, and cannot be otherwise.

VI. If a Creature is made by God, it must depend upon God, and receive all its Power from Him; with which Power the Creature can do nothing contrary to the Will of God, because God is Almighty; what is not contrary to His Will, must be agreeable to it; what is agreeable to it, must be good, because He is Good; therefore a Creature can do nothing but what is good.

This Proposition is much to the same Purpose with the former, but more particular; and its Conclusion is as just and evident. Tho' a Creature may do many Actions which by his Fellow Creatures will be nam'd Evil, and which will naturally and necessarily cause or bring upon the Doer, certain Pains (which will likewise be call'd Punishments;) yet this Proposition proves, that he cannot act what will be in itself really Ill, or displeasing to God. And that the painful Consequences of his evil Actions (so call'd) are not, as indeed they ought not to be, Punishments or Unhappinesses, will be shewn hereafter.

Nevertheless, the late learned Author of The Religion of Nature, (which I send you herewith) has given us a Rule or Scheme, whereby to discover which of our Actions ought to be esteem'd and denominated good, and which evil: It is in short this, "Every Action which is done according to Truth, is good; and every Action contrary to Truth, is evil: To act according to Truth is to use and esteem every Thing as what it is, &c. Thus if A steals a Horse from B, and rides away upon him, he uses him not as what he is in Truth, viz. the Property of another, but as his own, which is contrary to Truth, and therefore evil". But, as this Gentleman himself says, (Sect. I. Prop. VI.) "In order to judge rightly what any Thing is, it must be consider'd, not only what it is in one Respect, but also what it may be in any other Respect; and the whole Description of the Thing ought to be taken in:" So in this Case it ought to be consider'd, that A is naturally a covetous Being, feeling an Uneasiness in the want of B's Horse, which produces an Inclination for stealing him, stronger than his Fear of Punishment for so doing. This is Truth likewise, and A acts according to it when he steals the Horse. Besides, if it is prov'd to be a Truth, that A has not Power over his own Actions, it will be indisputable that he acts according to Truth, and impossible he should do otherwise.

I would not be understood by this to encourage or defend Theft; 'tis only for the sake of the Argument, and will certainly have no ill Effect. The Order and Course of Things will not be affected by Reasoning of this Kind; and 'tis as just and necessary, and as much according to Truth, for B to dislike and punish the Theft of his Horse, as it is for A to steal him.

VII. If the Creature is thus limited in his Actions, being able to do only such Things as God would have him to do, and not being able to refuse doing what God would have done; then he can have no such Thing as Liberty, Free-will or Power to do or refrain an Action.

By Liberty is sometimes understood the Absence of Opposition; and in this Sense, indeed, all our Actions may be said to be the Effects of our Liberty: But it is a Liberty of the same Nature with the Fall of a heavy Body to the Ground; it has Liberty to fall, that is, it meets with nothing to hinder its Fall, but at the same Time it is necessitated to fall, and has no Power or Liberty to remain suspended.

But let us take the Argument in another View, and suppose ourselves to be, in the common sense of the Word, Free Agents. As Man is a Part of this great Machine, the Universe, his regular Acting is requisite to the regular moving of the whole. Among the many Things which lie before him to be done, he may, as he is at Liberty and his Choice influenc'd by nothing, (for so it must be, or he is not at Liberty) chuse any one, and refuse the rest. Now there is every Moment something best to be done, which is alone then good, and with respect to which, every Thing else is at that Time evil. In order to know which is best to be done, and which not, it is requisite that we should have at one View all the intricate Consequences of every Action with respect to the general Order and Scheme of the Universe, both present and future; but they are innumerable and incomprehensible by any Thing but Omniscience. As we cannot know these, we have but as one Chance to ten thousand, to hit on the right Action; we should then be perpetually blundering about in the Dark, and putting the Scheme in Disorder; for every wrong Action of a Part, is a Defect or Blemish in the Order of the Whole. Is it not necessary then, that our Actions should be over-rul'd and govern'd by an all-wise Providence? -- How exact and regular is every Thing in the natural World! How wisely in every Part contriv'd! We cannot here find the least Defect! Those who have study'd the mere animal and vegetable Creation, demonstrate that nothing can be more harmonious and beautiful! All the heavenly Bodies, the Stars and Planets, are regulated with the utmost Wisdom! And can we suppose less Care to be taken in the Order of the moral than in the natural System? It is as if an ingenious Artificer, having fram'd a curious Machine or Clock, and put its many intricate Wheels and Powers in such a Dependance on one another, that the whole might move in the most exact Order and Regularity, had nevertheless plac'd in it several other Wheels endu'd with an independent Self-Motion, but ignorant of the general Interest of the

Clock; and these would every now and then be moving wrong, disordering the true Movement, and making continual Work for the Mender; which might better be prevented, by depriving them of that Power of Self-Motion, and placing them in a Dependance on the regular Part of the Clock.

VIII. If there is no such Thing as Free-Will in Creatures, there can be neither Merit nor Demerit in Creatures.

IX. And therefore every Creature must be equally esteem'd by the Creator.

These Propositions appear to be the necessary Consequences of the former. And certainly no Reason can be given, why the Creator should prefer in his Esteem one Part of His Works to another, if with equal Wisdom and Goodness he design'd and created them all, since all Ill or Defect, as contrary to his Nature, is excluded by his Power. We will sum up the Argument thus, When the Creator first design'd the Universe, either it was His Will and Intention that all Things should exist and be in the Manner they are at this Time; or it was his Will they should be otherwise i. e. in a different Manner: To say it was His Will Things should be otherwise than they are, is to say Somewhat hath contradicted His Will, and broken His Measures, which is impossible because inconsistent with his Power; therefore we must allow that all Things exist now in a Manner agreeable to His Will, and in consequence of that are all equally Good, and therefore equally esteem'd by Him.

I proceed now to shew, that as all the Works of the Creator are equally esteem'd by Him, so they are, as in Justice they ought to be, equally us'd.

SECT. II. Of Pleasure and Pain.

I. When a Creature is form'd and endu'd with Life, 'tis suppos'd to receive a Capacity of the Sensation of Uneasiness or Pain.

It is this distinguishes Life and Consciousness from unactive unconscious Matter. To know or be sensible of Suffering or being acted upon is to live; and whatsoever is not so, among created Things, is properly and truly dead.

All Pain and Uneasiness proceeds at first from and is caus'd by Somewhat without and distinct from the Mind itself. The Soul must first be acted upon before it can re-act. In the Beginning of Infancy it is as if it were not; it is not conscious of its own Existence, till it has receiv'd the first Sensation of Pain; then, and not before, it begins to feel itself, is rous'd, and put into Action; then it discovers its Powers and Faculties, and exerts them to expel the Uneasiness. Thus is the Machine set on work; this is Life. We are first mov'd by Pain, and the whole succeeding Course of our Lives is but one continu'd Series of Action with a View to be freed from it. As fast as we have excluded one Uneasiness another appears, otherwise the Motion would cease. If a continual Weight is not apply'd, the Clock will stop. And as soon as the Avenues of Uneasiness to the Soul are choak'd up or cut off, we are dead, we think and act no more.

II. This Uneasiness, whenever felt, produces Desire to be freed from it, great in exact proportion to the Uneasiness.

Thus is Uneasiness the first Spring and Cause of all Action; for till we are uneasy in Rest, we can have no Desire to move, and without Desire of moving there can be no voluntary Motion. The Experience of every Man who has observ'd his own Actions will evince the Truth of this; and I think nothing need be said to prove that the Desire will be equal to the Uneasiness, for the very Thing implies as much: It is not Uneasiness unless we desire to be freed from it, nor a great Uneasiness unless the consequent Desire is great.

I might here observe, how necessary a Thing in the Order and Design of the Universe this Pain or Uneasiness is, and how beautiful in its Place! Let us but suppose it just now banish'd the World entirely, and consider the Consequence of it: All the Animal Creation would immediately stand stock still, exactly in the Posture they were in the Moment Uneasiness departed; not a Limb, not a Finger would henceforth move; we should all be reduc'd to the Condition of Statues, dull and unactive: Here I should continue to sit motionless with the Pen in my Hand thus ------ and neither leave my Seat nor write one Letter more. This may appear odd at first View, but a little Consideration will make it evident; for 'tis impossible to assign any other Cause for the voluntary Motion of an Animal than its uneasiness in Rest. What a different Appearance then would the Face of Nature make, without it! How necessary is it! And how unlikely that the Inhabitants of the World ever were, or that the Creator ever design'd they should be, exempt from it!

I would likewise observe here, that the VIIIth Proposition in the preceding Section, viz. That there is neither Merit nor Demerit, &c. is here again demonstrated, as infallibly, tho' in another manner: For since Freedom from Uneasiness is the End of all our Actions, how is it possible for us to do any Thing disinterested? -- How can any Action be meritorious of Praise or Dispraise, Reward or Punishment, when the natural Principle of Self-Love is the only and the irresistible Motive to it?

III. This Desire is always fulfill'd or satisfy'd,

In the Design or End of it, tho' not in the Manner: The first is requisite, the latter not. To exemplify this, let us make a Supposition; A Person is confin'd in a House which appears to be in imminent Danger of Falling, this, as soon as perceiv'd, creates a violent Uneasiness, and that instantly produces an equal strong Desire, the End of which is freedom from the Uneasiness, and the Manner or Way propos'd to gain this End, is to get out of the House. Now if he is convinc'd by any Means, that he is mistaken, and the

House is not likely to fall, he is immediately freed from his Uneasiness, and the End of his Desire is attain'd as well as if it had been in the Manner desir'd, viz. leaving the House.

All our different Desires and Passions proceed from and are reducible to this one Point, Uneasiness, tho' the Means we propose to ourselves for expelling of it are infinite. One proposes Fame, another Wealth, a third Power, &c. as the Means to gain this End; but tho' these are never attain'd, if the Uneasiness be remov'd by some other Means, the Desire is satisfy'd. Now during the Course of Life we are ourselves continually removing successive Uneasinesses as they arise, and the last we suffer is remov'd by the sweet Sleep of Death.

IV. The fulfilling or Satisfaction of this Desire, produces the Sensation of Pleasure, great or small in exact proportion to the Desire.

Pleasure is that Satisfaction which arises in the Mind upon, and is caus'd by, the accomplishment of our Desires, and by no other Means at all; and those Desires being above shewn to be caus'd by our Pains or Uneasinesses, it follows that Pleasure is wholly caus'd by Pain, and by no other Thing at all.

V. Therefore the Sensation of Pleasure is equal, or in exact proportion to the Sensation of Pain.

As the Desire of being freed from Uneasiness is

equal to the Uneasiness, and the Pleasure of satisfying that Desire equal to the Desire, the Pleasure thereby produc'd must necessarily be equal to the Uneasiness or Pain which produces it: Of three Lines, A, B, and C, if A is equal to B, and B to C, C must be equal to A. And as our Uneasinesses are always remov'd by some Means or other, it follows that Pleasure and Pain are in their Nature inseparable: So many Degrees as one Scale of the Ballance descends, so many exactly the other ascends; and one cannot rise or fall without the Fall or Rise of the other: 'Tis impossible to taste of Pleasure, without feeling its preceding proportionate Pain; or to be sensible of Pain, without having its necessary Consequent Pleasure: The highest Pleasure is only Consciousness of Freedom from the deepest Pain, and Pain is not Pain to us unless we ourselves are sensible of it. They go Hand in Hand; they cannot be divided.

You have a View of the whole Argument in a few familiar Examples: The Pain of Abstinence from Food, as it is greater or less, produces a greater or less Desire of Eating, the Accomplishment of this Desire produces a greater or less Plcasurc proportionate to it. The Pain of Confinement causes the Desire of Liberty, which accomplish'd, yields a Pleasure equal to that Pain of Confinement. The Pain of Labour and Fatigue causes the Pleasure of Rest, equal to that Pain. The Pain of Absence from Friends, produces the Pleasure of Meeting in exact proportion. &c.

This is the fixt Nature of Pleasure and Pain, and

will always be found to be so by those who examine it.

One of the most common Arguments for the future Existence of the Soul, is taken from the generally suppos'd Inequality of Pain and Pleasure in the present; and this, notwithstanding the Difficulty by outward Appearances to make a Judgment of another's Happiness, has been look'd upon as almost unanswerable: but since Pain naturally and infallibly produces a Pleasure in proportion to it, every individual Creature must, in any State of Life, have an equal Quantity of each, so that there is not, on that Account, any Occasion for a future Adjustment.

Thus are all the Works of the Creator equally us'd by him; And no Condition of Life or Being is in itself better or preferable to another: The Monarch is not more happy than the Slave, nor the Beggar more miserable than Croesus. Suppose A, B, and C, three distinct Beings; A and B, animate, capable of Pleasure and Pain, C an inanimate Piece of Matter, insensible of either. A receives ten Degrees of Pain, which are necessarily succeeded by ten Degrees of Pleasure: B receives fifteen of Pain, and the consequent equal Number of Pleasure: C all the while lies unconcern'd, and as he has not suffer'd the former, has no right to the latter. What can be more equal and just than this? When the Accounts come to be adjusted, A has no Reason to complain that his Portion of Pleasure was five Degrees less than that of B, for his Portion of Pain was five Degrees less likewise: Nor has B any Reason to boast that his Pleasure was five Degrees greater than that of A, for his Pain was proportionate: They are then both on the same Foot with C, that is, they are neither Gainers nor Losers.

It will possibly be objected here, that even common Experience shews us, there is not in Fact this Equality: "Some we see hearty, brisk and chearful perpetually, while others are constantly burden'd with a heavy Load of Maladies and Misfortunes, remaining for Years perhaps in Poverty, Disgrace, or Pain, and die at last without any Appearance of Recompence." Now tho' 'tis not necessary, when a Proposition is demonstrated to be a general Truth, to shew in what manner it agrees with the particular Circumstances of Persons, and indeed ought not to be requir'd; yet, as this is a common Objection, some Notice may be taken of it: And here let it be observ'd, that we cannot be proper Judges of the good or bad Fortune of Others; we are apt to imagine, that what would give us a great Uneasiness or a great Satisfaction, has the same Effect upon others: we think, for Instance, those unhappy, who must depend upon Charity for a mean Subsistence, who go in Rags, fare hardly, and are despis'd and scorn'd by all; not considering that Custom renders all these Things easy, familiar, and even pleasant. When we see Riches, Grandeur and a chearful Countenance, we easily imagine Happiness accompanies them, when oftentimes 'tis quite otherwise: Nor is a constantly sorrowful Look, attended with continual Complaints, an infallible Indication of Unhappiness. In short, we can judge by nothing but Appearances, and they are very apt to deceive us. Some put on a gay chearful Outside, and appear to the World perfectly at Ease, tho' even then, some inward Sting, some secret Pain imbitters all their Joys, and makes the Ballance even: Others appear continually dejected and full of Sorrow; but even Grief itself is sometimes pleasant, and Tears are not always without their Sweetness: Besides, Some take a Satisfaction in being thought unhappy, (as others take a Pride in being thought humble,) these will paint their Misfortunes to others in the strongest Colours, and leave no Means unus'd to make you think them thoroughly miserable; so great a Pleasure it is to them to be pitied; Others retain the Form and outside Shew of Sorrow, long after the Thing itself, with its Cause, is remov'd from the Mind; it is a Habit they have acquir'd and cannot leave. These, with many others that might be given, are Reasons why we cannot make a true Estimate of the Equality of the Happiness and Unhappiness of others; and unless we could, Matter of Fact cannot be opposed to this Hypothesis. Indeed, we are sometimes apt to think, that the Uneasinesses we ourselves have had, outweigh our Pleasures; but the Reason is this, the Mind takes no Account of the latter, they slip away un-remark'd, when the former leave more lasting Impressions on the Memory. But suppose we pass the greatest part of Life in Pain and Sorrow, suppose we die by Torments and think no more, 'tis no Diminution to the Truth of what is here advanc'd; for the Pain, tho' exquisite, is not so to the last Moments of Life, the Senses are soon benumm'd, and render'd incapable of transmitting it so sharply to the Soul as at first; She perceives it cannot hold long, and 'tis an exquisite Pleasure to behold the immediate Approaches of Rest. This makes an Equivalent tho' Annihilation should follow: For the Quantity of Pleasure and Pain is not to be measur'd by its Duration, any more than the Quantity of Matter by its Extension; and as one cubic Inch may be made to contain, by Condensation, as much Matter as would fill ten thousand cubic Feet, being more expanded, so one single Moment of Pleasure may outweigh and compensate an Age of Pain.

It was owing to their Ignorance of the Nature of Pleasure and Pain that the Antient Heathens believ'd the idle Fable of their Elizium, that State of uninterrupted Ease and Happiness! The Thing is intirely impossible in Nature! Are not the Pleasures of the Spring made such by the Disagreeableness of the Winter? Is not the Pleasure of fair Weather owing to the Unpleasantness of foul? Certainly. Were it then always Spring, were the Fields always green and flourishing, and the Weather constantly serene and fair, the Pleasure would pall and die upon our Hands; it would cease to be Pleasure to us, when it is not usher'd in by Uneasiness. Could the Philosopher visit, in reality, every Star and Planet with as much Ease and Swiftness as he can now visit their Ideas, and pass from one to another of them in the Imagination; it would be a Pleasure I grant; but it would be only in proportion to the Desire of accomplishing it, and that would be no greater than the Uneasiness suffer'd in the Want of it. The Accomplishment of a long and difficult Journey yields a great Pleasure; but if we could take a Trip to the Moon and back again, as frequently and with as much Ease as we can go and come from Market, the Satisfaction would be just the same.

The Immateriality of the Soul has been frequently made use of as an Argument for its Immortality; but let us consider, that tho' it should be allow'd to be immaterial, and consequently its Parts incapable of Separation or Destruction by any Thing material, yet by Experience we find, that it is not incapable of Cessation of Thought, which is its Action. When the Body is but a little indispos'd it has an evident Effect upon the Mind; and a right Disposition of the Organs is requisite to a right Manner of Thinking. In a sound Sleep sometimes, or in a Swoon, we cease to think at all; tho' the Soul is not therefore then annihilated, but exists all the while tho' it does not act; and may not this probably be the Case after Death? All our Ideas are first admitted by the Senses and imprinted on the Brain, increasing in Number by Observation and Experience; there they become the Subjects of the Soul's Action. The Soul is a mere Power or Faculty of contemplating on, and comparing those Ideas when it has them; hence springs Reason: But as it can think on nothing but Ideas, it must have them before it can think at all. Therefore as it may exist before it has receiv'd any Ideas, it may exist before it thinks. To remember a Thing, is to have the Idea of it still plainly imprinted on the Brain, which the Soul can turn to and contemplate on Occasion. To forget a Thing, is to have the Idea of it defac'd and destroy'd by some Accident, or the crouding in and imprinting of great variety of other Ideas upon it, so that the Soul cannot find out its Traces and distinguish it. When we have thus lost the Idea of any one Thing, we can think no more, or cease to think, on that Thing; and as we can lose the Idea of one Thing, so we may of ten, twenty, a hundred, &c. and even of all Things, because they are not in their Nature permanent; and often during Life we see that some Men, (by an Accident or Distemper affecting the Brain,) lose the greatest Part of their Ideas, and remember very little of their past Actions and Circumstances. Now upon Death, and the Destruction of the Body, the Ideas contain'd in the Brain, (which are alone the Subjects of the Soul's Action) being then likewise necessarily destroy'd, the Soul, tho' incapable of Destruction itself, must then necessarily cease to think or act, having nothing left to think or act upon. It is reduc'd to its first inconscious State before it receiv'd any Ideas. And to cease to think is but little different from ceasing to be.

Nevertheless, 'tis not impossible that this same Faculty of contemplating Ideas may be hereafter united to a new Body, and receive a new Set of Ideas; but that will no way concern us who are now living; for the Identity will be lost, it is no longer that same Self but a new Being.

I shall here subjoin a short Recapitulation of the Whole, that it may with all its Parts be comprehended at one View.

1. It is suppos'd that God the Maker and

Governour of the Universe, is infinitely wise, good, and powerful.

2. In consequence of His infinite Wisdom and Goodness, it is asserted, that whatever He doth must be infinitely wise and good;

3. Unless He be interrupted, and His Measures broken by some other Being, which is impossible because He is Almighty.

4. In consequence of His infinite Power, it is asserted, that nothing can exist or be done in the Universe which is not agreeable to His Will, and therefore good.

5. Evil is hereby excluded, with all Merit and Demerit; and likewise all preference in the Esteem of God, of one Part of the Creation to another. This is the Summary of the first Part.

Now our common Notions of Justice will tell us, that if all created Things are equally esteem'd by the Creator, they ought to be equally us'd by Him; and that they are therefore equally us'd, we might embrace for Truth upon the Credit, and as the true Consequence of the foregoing Argument. Nevertheless we proceed to confirm it, by shewing how they are equally us'd, and that in the following Manner.

1. A Creature when endu'd with Life or Consciousness, is made capable of Uneasiness or Pain.

2. This Pain produces Desire to be freed from it, in exact proportion to itself.

3. The Accomplishment of this Desire produces an equal Pleasure.

4. Pleasure is consequently equal to Pain.

From these Propositions it is observ'd,

1. That every Creature hath as much Pleasure as Pain.

2. That Life is not preferable to Insensibility; for Pleasure and Pain destroy one another: That Being which has ten Degrees of Pain subtracted from ten of Pleasure, has nothing remaining, and is upon an equality with that Being which is insensible of both.

3. As the first Part proves that all Things must be equally us'd by the Creator because equally esteem'd; so this second Part demonstrates that they are equally esteem'd because equally us'd.

4. Since every Action is the Effect of Self-Uneasiness, the Distinction of Virtue and Vice is excluded; and Prop. VIII. in Sect. I. again demonstrated.

5. No State of Life can be happier than the present, because Pleasure and Pain are inseparable.

Thus both Parts of this Argument agree with and confirm one another, and the Demonstration is reciprocal.

I am sensible that the Doctrine here advanc'd, if it were to be publish'd, would meet with but an indifferent Reception. Mankind naturally and generally love to be flatter'd: Whatever sooths our Pride, and tends to exalt our Species above the rest of the Creation, we are pleas'd with and easily believe, when ungrateful Truths shall be with the utmost Indignation rejected. "What! bring ourselves down to an Equality with the Beasts of the Field! with the meanest part of the Creation! 'Tis insufferable!" But, (to use a Piece of common Sense) our Geese are but Geese tho' we may think 'em Swans; and Truth will be Truth tho' it sometimes prove mortifying and distasteful.

London, 1725

THE END

RISE OF DOUAI

RISE OF DOUAI

TWITTER : @RISEOFDOUAI

 OTHER PUBLICATIONS:

- AN IDIOT'S GUIDE TO: BEE HUNTING BY JOHN LOCKARD, EDITED BY ARSALAN AHMED (2012)(PAPERBACK) ISBN-10: 1478383550

- THE RISE OF DOUAI BY ARSALAN AHMED (2012)(PAPERBACK) ISBN-10: 1479267783

- THE RICHEST MAN IN BABYLON BY GEORGE S. CLASON (2012) (PAPERBACK) ISBN-10: 1479377341

- THINK AND GROW RICH BY NAPOLEON HILL (2012) (PAPERBACK) ISBN-10: 1480061638

- AS A MAN THINKETH BY MR JAMES ALLEN (2012) (PAPERBACK) ISBN-10: 1480088161
- HOW TO ANALYZE PEOPLE ON

SIGHT BY ELSIE BENEDICT (PAPERBACK) ISBN-10: 1480081272

- THE ART OF WAR BY MR SUN TZU (PAPERBACK) ISBN-10: 1480082007
- MACBETH BY MR WILLIAM SHAKESPEARE (PAPERBACK) ISBN-10: 1480060682
- A CHRISTMAS CAROL BY MR CHARLES DICKENS ISBN-10: 1481194755
- CREATING CAPITAL: MONEY-MAKING AS AN AIM IN BUSINESS BY MR FREDRICK L LIPMAN ISBN-10: 1481158996
- GETTING GOLD: A PRACTICAL TREATISE FOR PROSPECTORS, MINERS, AND STUDENTS BY MR JOSEPH COLIN FRANCIS JOHNSON ISBN-10: 1481090984
- THE INTERPRETATION OF DREAMS BY MR SIGMUND FREUD ISBN-10: 1481134558
- THE COMMUNIST MANIFESTO BY MR KARL MARX AND MR FRIDRICK ENGLES ISBN-10:

1480112445

- THE PRINCE BY MR NICCOLO MACHIAVELLI ISBN-10: 1480119601
- THE WAY TO WEALTH BY MR BENJAMIN FRANKLIN ISBN-10: 1480099651
- THE ART OF MONEY GETTING - OR GOLDEN RULES FOR MAKING MONEY (SUCCESS PRINCIPLES) BY MR PHINEAS TAYLOR BARNUM ISBN-10: 1480138622

Twitter : **@RiseofDouai**

26482018R00020

Made in the USA
Lexington, KY
22 December 2018

A Dissertation on Liberty and Necessity, Pleasure and Pain

A Dissertation on Liberty and Necessity, Pleasure and Pain is an essay by Benjamin Franklin, a founder of the United States. A noted polymath, Franklin was a leading author, printer, political theorist, politician, postmaster, scientist, musician, inventor, satirist, civic activist, statesman, and diplomat. As a scientist, he was a major figure in the American Enlightenment and the history of physics for his discoveries and theories regarding electricity. He invented the lightning rod, bifocals, the Franklin stove, a carriage odometer, and the glass 'armonica'. He facilitated many civic organizations, including a fire department and a university.

About the Author

Franklin earned the title of "The First American" for his early and indefatigable campaigning for colonial unity; as an author and spokesman in London for several colonies, then as the first United States Ambassador to France, he exemplified the emerging American nation. Franklin was foundational in defining the American ethos as a marriage of the practical values of thrift, hard work, education, community spirit, self-governing institutions, and opposition to authoritarianism both political and religious, with the scientific and tolerant values of the Enlightenment. In the words of historian Henry Steele Commager, "In a Franklin could be merged the virtues of Puritanism without its defects, the illumination of the Enlightenment without its heat." To Walter Isaacson, this makes Franklin "the most accomplished American of his age and the most influential in inventing the type of society America would become."